WRONG WAY, JONAH!

JONAH

KAY ARTHUR
WITH SCOTI DOMEIJ

HARVEST HOUSE PUBLISHERS
Eugene, Oregon 97402

All Scripture quotations are taken from the New American Standard Bible, © 1960, 1962, 1963, 1968, 1971, 1972, 1973, 1975, 1977, 1995 by The Lockman Foundation. Used by permission.

Illustrations by Steve Bjorkman

Cover by Left Coast Design, Portland, Oregon

Discover 4 Yourself® Inductive Bible Studies for Kids

WRONG WAY, JONAH!

Copyright © 1999 by Precept Ministries International
Published by Harvest House Publishers
Eugene, Oregon 97402
www.harvesthousepublishers.com

ISBN-13: 978-0-7369-0203-8
ISBN-10: 0-7369-0203-1

CONTENTS

Getting the Story from God's Word:
A Bible Study *You* Can Do!

GETTING THE STORY FROM GOD'S WORD

A BIBLE STUDY YOU CAN DO!

There's a big news story unfolding in Israel! It has something to do with their old enemy Assyria—and we at the *Testimony Times* need the scoop! We need to know what's going on and why, who's involved, and what all the commotion means. And we want to be the first to print the story!

This is a big assignment for a rookie reporter, but we know you can do it! You have exactly what you need: God's Word in your hands and God's Spirit to help you understand it.

Besides, the book that you're holding is designed to help you get the story—and understand what it means for you! It's called an inductive Bible study. That word *inductive* means that this Bible study is set up to help you investigate the book of Jonah and discover for yourself what it means. Instead of reading what someone else says the story means, you'll look at the Bible passages and figure it out for yourself.

So your assignment is to stick close to Jonah (we'll cover your travel expenses), interview the people he knew (you'll definitely meet some interesting folks), and let us know what happens as it happens (all the materials you need are right here).

If you're ready, let's get started!

THINGS YOU'LL NEED
▼

NEW AMERICAN STANDARD BIBLE (UPDATED EDITION)
PEN OR PENCIL
COLORED PENCILS FOR OBSERVATION WORKSHEETS
INDEX CARDS
A DICTIONARY
THIS WORKBOOK

1

JONAH 1

Your Assignment

When news stories break, a lot can happen in a little bit of time. So as you dig into the story of Jonah, keep your wits about you. We're sure that with God's help you'll be able to gather the facts, write a super story, and even learn some lessons for life.

In fact, before your assignment on the Joppa-Nineveh news desk is over, you'll learn a lot about Jonah and about God. And we look forward to the reporting you'll do for the readers of *Testimony Times*. Get to work! We want to scoop the competition and be the first with the story.

One more thing. Along the way you'll find activities labeled "Extra! Extra!" These aren't necessary for you to get the facts for the *Testimony Times*, but they're a great chance for you to have fun and learn more.

▼

GETTING YOUR BEARINGS

Have you ever thought you knew something—and then found out you weren't quite right? Well, investigative reporters need to be accurate! We don't want hunches: We want the story told as it happened. After all, people are counting on you to give them the facts.

So before you start to track down Jonah, list three things you've heard from others about what happened to him. While you're on assignment, you'll see if they were right!

1. _____

2. _____

3. _____

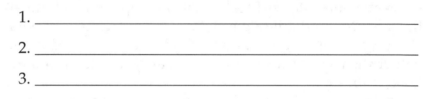

A WORD TO OUR NEW REPORTER

Each week on this assignment you'll have a memory verse. It will give you direction as you do your investigative work. Here's the verse for this week.

For I know that the Lord is great
And that our Lord is above all gods.
Whatever the Lord pleases, He does,
In heaven and in earth, in the seas and in all the
    deeps.
                    — Psalm 135:5-6

Now write Psalm 135:5-6 on an index card so you can carry

it with you. Read it out loud at least three times each day. Your goal is to memorize this verse by the end of the week.

What are three things your memory verse tells you about God?

1. _____

2. _____

3. _____

Has anything in your life made you think that "the Lord is great"? List two or three of those things.

_____

_____

_____

Where does the Lord do whatever He pleases?

_____

HEADLINE NEWS

A great way to tackle any assignment for the Lord is to start by praying, and your investigative report is no exception. Your Bible is the source for the information you need, and it's important to ask God to help you understand what you find there. So ask God to help you get the facts straight and then read through Jonah 1. It starts on page 89 of this book.

Reporters need to get the reader's attention, and a good headline is key. In newspaper talk, "head" is short for "headline" and refers to the title of the story. The "head" lets the reader know what the story is about in just a few words. Write a "head" for Jonah 1.

_____

Investigative reporters need to identify the main people and the most important events in the story they're writing. One way you can do this is by looking for words that pop up again and again.

We call those *key words* because they unlock the meaning of the Bible passage and give you the facts you need for writing your story.

Key words offer you clues about what is most important in a passage of Scripture. Taking the time to mark them will help you figure out for yourself what the Bible is teaching.

KEY WORDS
✓ Key words are usually used over and over again
✓ Key words are important
✓ Key words are used by the writer for a reason

Now turn to page 89. We call these pages "Observation Worksheets," and this is where you'll do your investigative work. Today, you'll focus on Jonah 1:1-9. As you read these nine verses again, look for and mark the key words listed below.

Here are some helpful ways to mark these words. You may mark them by using different colors instead of symbols. Different colors are easier to spot quickly. However, if you want to use symbols, remember to keep them simple. You can use ours or make up your own.

By the way, you also need to mark the pronouns that refer to each one of the key words.

Jonah (orange)   Lord or Lord God (yellow)

sailors (dark blue)   captain (blue and red)

calamity (red)

Good job! You've found some important clues. Tomorrow we'll start figuring out what they tell us!

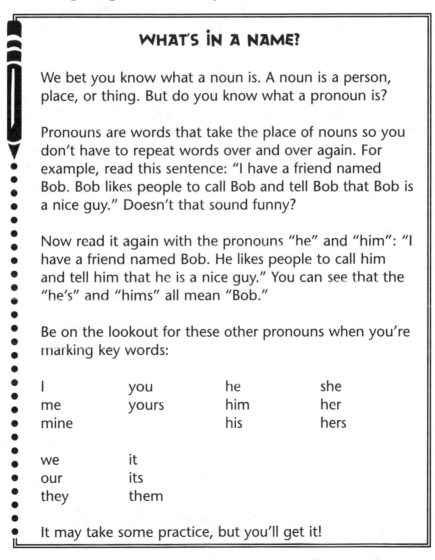

WHAT'S IN A NAME?

We bet you know what a noun is. A noun is a person, place, or thing. But do you know what a pronoun is?

Pronouns are words that take the place of nouns so you don't have to repeat words over and over again. For example, read this sentence: "I have a friend named Bob. Bob likes people to call Bob and tell Bob that Bob is a nice guy." Doesn't that sound funny?

Now read it again with the pronouns "he" and "him": "I have a friend named Bob. He likes people to call him and tell him that he is a nice guy." You can see that the "he's" and "hims" all mean "Bob."

Be on the lookout for these other pronouns when you're marking key words:

I	you	he	she
me	yours	him	her
mine		his	hers

we	it
our	its
they	them

It may take some practice, but you'll get it!

▼

WAY WRONG, JONAH!

Don't try to tackle your big assignment today without praying or reviewing your memory verse. Okay, let's go!

The 5Ws and an H

The "5Ws and an H" is an odd phrase that refers to the questions "WHO?" "WHAT?" "WHERE?" "WHEN?" "WHY?" and "HOW?" A well-written article will answer those questions for the reader. In fact, the lead (or opening sentence) will include answers to as many of those questions as possible, and the paragraphs that follow will give more details.

Look again at Jonah 1:1-9.

Jonah 1:1 WHO is the main person in this story?

_____

Jonah 1:2 WHAT two things did God tell Jonah to do?

_____

_____

Jonah 1:2 WHY did God want Jonah to go to Nineveh?

_____

Jonah 1:3 HOW did Jonah respond to God's command?

_____

Jonah 1:4 WHAT did God do when Jonah tried to run from His presence?

_____

That's a lot of action in just a few verses! Already the story is exciting! But the story will mean more if you understand (and explain to your readers) something about where all this action is taking place.

Jonah's Flight Plan

Turn again to your Observation Worksheet. Draw two green lines under the names of these cities every time you see them:

Nineveh   Tarshish   Joppa

As a reporter who wants to get all the facts, this is a good way to mark anything that tells you WHERE. Now look at this map.

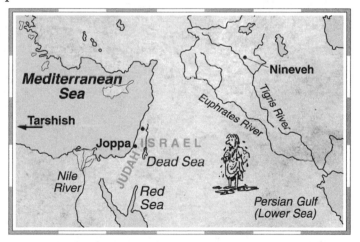

Jonah 1:2 WHERE did God tell Jonah to go?

_____

Draw a green arrow from Jonah to the city God told him to go.

Jonah 1:3 WHERE did Jonah go to instead?

_____

Draw a red arrow from Jonah to the seaport city where he bought a ticket for a boat ride.

Jonah 1:3 WHERE was the boat going to?

_____

Now draw another red arrow from Joppa to where the ship was going to take Jonah.

Which way was Jonah going? The right way or the wrong way? How do you know?

Can you think of a time when you knew the right thing to do but didn't do it? Write out a brief story about what you did. What happened? What should you have done?

WRONG WAY, _____ **!**
                       (put your name here)

_____

_____

_____

_____

Jonah went the wrong way when he headed out for Joppa instead of Nineveh. Not a great start on his mission from God! But you're off to a super start in your assignment to track this story! Keep up the good work!

LOTS TO DO

Take a moment to remember what was happening when we left Jonah.

Jonah 1:2 WHERE did God want Jonah to go?

_____

Jonah 1:3 WHERE was Jonah during the sea voyage?

_____

Jonah 1:4 WHAT were the weather conditions?

_____

NINEVEH—THEN AND NOW

Nineveh was the capital city of the nation of Assyria, a longtime enemy of Israel. For more than 100 years, the Assyrians continually attacked the borders and raided the land. The Assyrians were fierce warriors who either killed or tortured the people they defeated—and that included the Jews.

Nineveh itself was a large city (it took three days to walk through it) located on the east bank of the Tigris River. It was built at the main river crossing leading to the best farmland. The wall that surrounded the city was 50 feet high. Ninevah was also home to many beautiful temples built to false gods. The people's idol worship made God angry.

The ruins of Nineveh are in the modern-day country of Iraq.

Now for more details.

Jonah 1:5 HOW did the sailors respond to the storm?

_____

Jonah 1:5 WHAT was Jonah doing as the storm raged?

_____

Jonah 1:6 WHAT instructions does the captain give Jonah?

_____

Jonah 1:7 WHAT do the sailors do to figure out why they were in such a nasty storm?

_____

Jonah 1:7 WHO did the lots fall on?

_____

Jonah 1:8 WHAT did the sailors want to know about Jonah?

_____

Jonah 1:9 WHAT did Jonah say? WHAT did he leave out? (Remember verse 2!)

_____

_____

CASTING LOTS

In the Old Testament, people cast lots to decide things. God sometimes used lots to reveal truth to His people. In the New Testament God gave His people different ways to know the truth, by reading His Word and obeying the leaders He had appointed over them.

Lots were small bits of wood or stone. Sometimes the names of people were written on the stones. The stones were placed in a container and shaken together. The first "lot" to fall out showed who was chosen. When the sailors cast lots, who was identified? Right! The storm had struck because of Jonah.

Let's see what your key words help reveal about this passage of Scripture.

What key word does verse 7 contain?

_____

What do you think "calamity" means? Use a dictionary to confirm your guess.

_____

Now investigate the text! Read Jonah 1:1-9. What is the calamity? How is it described in Jonah 1:4?

_____

Mark these words the same way you marked the key words.

A picture is worth a thousand words! And it gets our attention quickly. In Jonah's day they didn't have cameras so they had to draw pictures. Instead of taking a photo, draw a picture of what you've seen in Jonah 1:1-9. We plan to run the drawing with your piece—and the right "shot" will make your story impossible to skip!

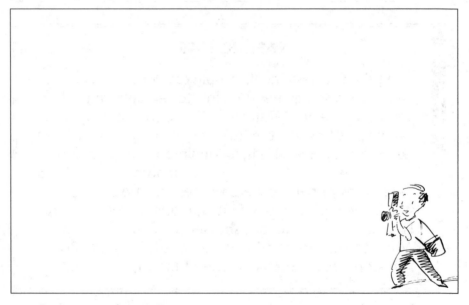

One more thing. Practice your memory verse by reading it or trying to say it without looking at your card. What evidence that "whatever [the Lord] pleases, He does" have you seen in Jonah 1:1-9?

_____

_____

▼

GOING TO PRESS

The deadline approaches! We need to get the story printed, and we know you're almost ready to send it our way!

A few days ago when you first read through Jonah 1, you wrote a head for the chapter. Write that title here.

_____

To keep the reader's interest and move the story along in bite-sized pieces, journalists often write subheads for different sections of their story. Since this is the first piece of your ongoing story, come up with another head for Jonah 1:1-9. Write it at the top of your story on p. 18.

Look again at the photo you drew yesterday. It's time to fill in the holes of your story.

TESTIMONY TIMES

ISSUE 1   VOL 1

BIG NEWS!

Put your headline here.

Although commanded by

_____
whom (Jonah 1:1)

to go to

_____
where (verse 2)

to

_____ ,
what (verse 2)

the prophet

_____
who (verse 1)

headed instead for a seaport in Joppa. After buying a ticket for Tarshish, he climbed aboard the ship and went down into its hold. Sources say Jonah was trying to flee from

_____ .
whom (verse 3)

Not long into the voyage a great calamity happened.

A violent

_____
what (verse 4)

struck. Sailors threw cargo overboard to lighten the load and save the ship and their lives. When the storm didn't stop, they decided to cast

_____
what (verse 7)

_____ .
why (verse 7)

When the lot fell to

_____ ,
whom (verse 7)

the sailors asked him many questions. As the waves crashed and wind howled, Jonah responded, "I am a Hebrew, and I fear

_____
whom (verse 9)

who made the sea and the dry land."

Great story! You'll have readers looking forward to the next report!

"EXTRA! EXTRA!"

Give Us a Hand!

Your story was so good, you may want to get some of your friends and turn it into a TV show.

As you read either Jonah 1:1-9 from the Bible or the story you wrote before or as you tell of the events in your own words, use hand motions and sound effects to illustrate what is happening. What will the rain sound like? How will you make the noise of the wind? What gestures suggest Jonah is running? Now you're ready to put your show on for your family or neighbors. Have fun! We'll add more later!

2

Jonah 1:10-17

Your Assignment

Your story is off to a great start. You're helping us sell papers! Keep up the good work this week!

GETTING YOUR BEARINGS

In his daily log, the captain of a ship keeps track of important events on the journey. When tragedies or problems happen at sea, a good reporter will try to get ahold of the Captain's log. Read Jonah 1:10-17 on your Observation Worksheet (pages 89-90) and let's see what the captain could have written in his log about what has been happening on this voyage to Tarshish. Help him fill it in.

Crew's Concerns/Activities

1:10-11 _____

Weather Report

1:11_____

Passenger Activity

1:12_____

Crew's Concerns/Activities

1:13_____

Crew's Concerns/Activities

1:14 _____

Events

1:15_____

Unusual Happenings

1:15 _____

Crew's Concerns/Activities

1:16 _____

Unusual Happenings

1:17 _____

CALL COLLECT

As the story of Jonah unfolds this week and next, we think you'll figure out why we chose these verses for you to memorize!

> The Lord is near to all who call upon Him,
>   To all who call upon Him in truth.
> He will fulfill the desire of those who fear Him;
>   He will also hear their cry and will save them.
>   — Psalm 145:18-19

Write this passage on an index card—or two! The passage breaks after the second line. Having two cards may help the memorization go more easily for you!

DAY 2

THE OLD HEAVE HO

There's a lot to learn as you get ready to write your next piece in the Jonah story. Let's get to it!

Keys to Understanding

List your key words below (we've given a few clues!), and finish marking them in verses 10-17 of Jonah 1. Next to each write down one thing you learn about each key word from reading the first chapter of Jonah.

__ __ N __ __   _____

__ O __ __   _____

S__ __ __ __ __ S   _____

__ A __ __ A __ __   _____

__ A __ A __ __ __ __ _____

    Also, this week, look for the key word "pray" and its synonym "called." Do you know what a *synonym* is?

    Synonyms give a story more description, interest, and action.

    Sometimes different words mean the same thing. For example, "sailboat," a "yacht" and a "dinghy" are all boats. These words are *synonyms!* Our key word today is "pray," but there is a synonym for the word "pray" in this chapter. It is "called." There are also some synonyms for "sailors." Can you find them?

pray (called)

THOSE 5 WS AND THAT H

    You'd be surprised by how much you can learn by asking the questions WHO, WHAT, WHERE, WHEN, WHY, and HOW.

    WHO helps you find out facts like who wrote this section of Scripture, who was it written for, who do we read about in it, and who did this or said that.

    WHAT helps you understand what the author is talking about and what main things happen in the passage.

    WHERE lets you learn where something happened, where people went, and where words were spoken.

    WHEN asks questions like "When did this event happen?" and "When did the main character do something?"

    WHY questions are ones like "Why did he say that?" and "Why did this happen?"

- **HOW** lets you figure out things like how something was done and how people knew something had happened.

As you study the Bible, you can learn a lot by asking the 5Ws and an H because the answers are right in God's Word! Answer these questions from Jonah 1:10-17.

Jonah 1:10   WHO was fleeing from the Lord? (If you need some help, read verse 2.)

_____

Jonah 1:12   WHAT did Jonah tell the sailors to do so that the sea would become calm?

_____

Jonah 1:13   WHERE did the men try to row the boat?

_____

Jonah 1:14   WHAT did the sailors pray?

_____

Jonah 1:15   WHEN did the storm calm down?

_____

Jonah 1:16   WHY did the crew of the boat offer sacrifices to God?

_____

_____

Jonah 1:17   HOW did the Lord preserve Jonah?

_____

Good investigating! We can see your story coming together! (By the way, what's this week's memory verse?)

FISHY BUSINESS

Details can make or break a story! They are the little facts and bits of information that make a story interesting. Ask God to help you find some interesting details as you read His Word.

Look back to Jonah 1:6.

WHAT did the captain tell Jonah to do?

_____

WHY did the captain want Jonah to pray?

_____

In Jonah 1:9 we find the word "God" with a capital G.

WHO is speaking in this verse?

_____

HOW did Jonah describe God?

_____

Read verse 10.

WHAT impossible thing was Jonah trying to do?

_____

Now look at verses 14, 15, and 16.

WHAT did the sailors pray?

_____

To WHOM did they pray?

_____

HOW did Jonah's God respond when the prophet was thrown into the sea?

_____

And HOW did the crew respond to God's demonstration of His power?

_____

Verse 17 is a bit of surprise ending to Jonah 1. Is that a switch? (Look at verse 6.)

WHAT happened?

_____

WHO caused that strange event?

_____

HOW long was Jonah in the belly of the fish?

_____

Before you call it a day, write a headline for Jonah 1:10-17.

_____

You're closing in on another hot story! Great work!

A WHALE OF A TALE

What kind of a "fish" swallowed Jonah? No one knows exactly. Many people speculate that it was a great white shark. A 19-foot shark can swallow a man whole. Large sperm whales have also been known to visit the Mediterranean Sea, where Jonah was caught in the storm. Sperm whales grow up to 65 feet long—plenty of room in there. Or it might just have been a big fish! Whatever it was, the Bible says God provided it especially to rescue Jonah!

DAY 4

▼

SAY CHEESE!

Before you get ready to prep your story for printing tomorrow, get the photo you'll need to send to the editor's desk. Below draw a picture from Jonah 1:10-17. Be sure to draw one that will add credibility to the amazing event you're about to report.

It's time to smooth out the rough edges of your draft and get that story off to type! But first a quick question: Any idea why we chose Psalm 145:18-19 as this week's memory verse? Maybe a quick review of the lines will help you take a guess! Fill in the blanks below. It would be great if you can do it from memory!

The Lord is _____ to all who _____ upon Him,

To all who _____ upon Him in _____ .

He will fulfill the _____ of those who _____ Him:

He will also _____ their cry and will _____ them.

                                    — Psalm 145:18-19

Who in Jonah 1 might find the promise of Psalm 145:18-19 especially comforting?

_____

Has there ever been a time when you cried to God and He helped you?

_____

_____

GOING TO PRESS

They're warming up the presses, and they're waiting for your story! Now write in the line below the headline you came up with for Jonah 1:10-17.

_____

TESTIMONY TIMES

ISSUE 2   VOL 2

BIG NEWS!

Put your headline here.

When we last left Jonah, the storm was raging as he explained to the ship's crew that he was a Hebrew who served the God who made the sea.

Aware that

_____
who (Jonah 1:3)

was fleeing from God, the sailors were

_____
what (Jonah 1:10)

and wanted to know

_____ .
what (Jonah 1:10)

When Jonah told them to

_____ ,
what (Jonah 1:12)

the crew tried instead to row

_____ .
where (Jonah 1:13)

When they realized they couldn't succeed, they

_____ .
what (Jonah 1:14)

Then, despite their initial rejection of Jonah's proposal, the sailors

_____ .
what, who, where (Jonah 1:15)

Instantly, the storm stopped—and just as quickly the men

_____ .
what (Jonah 1:16)

What happened next was even more amazing than the end of the storm and the prayers of the crew.

_____
who (Jonah 1:17)

appointed

_____
what (Jonah 1:17)

to

_____ .
what, who (Jonah 1:17)

Reliable eyewitnesses report that Jonah was

_____ .
where, when (Jonah 1:17)

Wow! What an exciting story that was. It's not every day that a man gets swallowed by a big fish. There was something special about this fish. *God appointed it!* That means God picked it out and sent it just to save Jonah. Even though Jonah had disobeyed God, God still helped him by sending the fish so he wouldn't drown. It's kind of like God sending Jesus to save us even though we disobeyed God. God had big plans for Jonah. He has big plans for you, too, if you'll decide to follow Jesus and love Him with all your heart. Think about it. Talk to God about it.

Well, you've done another good job! Readers of the *Testimony Times* are glad you're on the Joppa-Nineveh beat!

"EXTRA! EXTRA!"

Raindrop Art

Gather empty salt shakers or spice bottles, powdered tempera paint, poster board, spray bottles, crayons, and newspapers or an old shower curtain.

1. Fill the salt shakers or spice bottles with dry tempera paint.
2. Cover your work area with newspapers or the old shower curtain.
3. Use your crayons to draw a scene from Jonah 1 on the poster board.
4. Shake the powdered paint over the picture.
5. Fill your spray bottle with water and then spray the picture.
6. Let the paint dry and then shake off excess paint.

Give Us a Hand!

More action calls for more hand motions and maybe more sound effects! As you read either Jonah 1:10-17 from the Bible or the story you wrote or as you tell of the events in your own words, add hand motions and sound effects. Have fun!

3

JONAH 2

Your Assignment

What's the first thing to do? Pray! And that's extra important when the person you're writing about is inside the belly of a fish. It's a tricky writing assignment, but we know you'll do great!

GETTING YOUR BEARINGS

You're entering the next leg of your investigative journey, and that means new material. After praying for God's blessing on your efforts, read the last verse of Jonah 1 again. Where's Jonah? What's happening?

As a good reporter and journalist, it's your job to find out. Now turn to your Observation Worksheet on page 90 and read Jonah 2. Take your pen and mark or color every reference to Jonah. After his name is mentioned once, you have to look for the pronouns that are substituted for Jonah's name. Watch for every "he," "I," "me," or "my" that belongs to Jonah and mark those in the same way.

Jonah 2:1 WHAT is Jonah doing as Chapter 2 begins?

_____

Jonah 2:1 WHY do you think Jonah is doing that?

_____

Do you think that's a good idea? _____ WHY?

_____

The last WHAT question is answered more completely by other key words you'll find in Jonah 2. Turn to your Observation Worksheet starting on page 90 and mark the key word "pray" and its synonyms "called" and "cried" in Jonah 2.

Now using the same color you used to mark *Lord God* in Jonah 1, mark *Lord* as well as the pronouns *He, You,* and *Your.* Pronouns are words that are used so you don't have to keep repeating a name. When Jonah prayed to God, instead of using God's name all the time he used the pronouns "He," "You," and "Your." When you mark a key word like "Lord God," be sure to mark all of the pronouns too.

So mark:

pray *or* prayed (called, cried)   Lord (pronouns: He, You, Your)

We'll get back to these key words soon! Time out right now for . . .

A PRAYER FROM THE DEEP

Jonah propbably wasn't very happy to be in the belly of the fish. But he knew what he should do. . . pray to God. This week you're going to memorize part of Jonah's prayer!

> I will sacrifice to You
> With the voice of thanksgiving.
> That which I have vowed I will pay.
> Salvation is from the Lord.
> —Jonah 2:9

DAY 2

GETTING THE SCOOP

It's every reporter's dream to be able to listen to or talk to the very people that the story is about! To be the very first reporter to get the story written and printed is to get what's called a "scoop" in newspaper talk. So let's get the scoop on this fish tale!

Turn to Jonah 2 and notice what Jonah does. We've given you a headstart.

Jonah 2:1   P __ __ __ __ __

Jonah 2:2   C __ __ __ __ __

            C __ __ __ __

Jonah 2:4   E __ __ __ __ __ __ __

Jonah 2:6   D __ __ __ __ __ __ __ __

Jonah 2:7   R __ __ __ __ __ __ __ __ __

Jonah 2:9   WILL S __ __ __ __ __ __ __ __

WHAT does God do in each of the following verses? Again, we've given you a headstart in your answers.

Jonah 2:2   A __ __ __ __ __ __ __

                 H __ __ __ __

Jonah 2:3   C __ __ __

Jonah 2:6   B __ __ __ __ __ __

Jonah 2:10   C __ __ __ __ __ __ __ __

Jonah 2:3   WHAT did God do?

_____

Jonah 1:3   HOW had Jonah disobeyed God?

_____

Jonah 1:15 WHO threw Jonah overboard?

_____

But according to Jonah 2:3, WHO allowed it?

_____

Did God want Jonah to die when He allowed the sailors to throw Jonah into the sea?   Yes   No   (circle one.)

HOW do you know? Look at Jonah 1:17. WHAT did God do?

_____

_____

HOW did God turn Jonah around when he was going the wrong way? See what Jonah 2:10 says.

_____

Isn't God awesome? Even in the belly of the fish, Jonah realized that it was God who put him there and only God could get him out.

Did you see the "then" in Jonah 2:10? Words like "then," "before," "after," and "the next day" tell us WHEN something happened. It's good to mark WHEN words by drawing a clock in the margin next to them so you can spot them quickly. Mark the "then" that you saw on your Observation Worksheet.

Jonah 2:7 WHAT did Jonah do *before* God commanded the fish to vomit?

_____

_____

WHY is Jonah—who is sitting in the belly of a fish—so thankful? (Hint 2:5. What could have happened to Jonah in the stormy seas?)

_____

_____

WHY might Jonah have been less than thankful? (Hints: Jonah 1:17 and 2:1.)

_____

_____

It's often easier to look at the little picture ("I'm stuck in the stomach of this fish!") than the big picture ("I don't know when I'm going to get out of here or how, but God must have a plan for me since He didn't let me drown in that storm."). Maybe you're worried or sad about something right now. Maybe somebody started a club or had a party and you weren't invited. You can learn a lesson from Jonah's example. He found reasons to give thanks to God—from the belly of a fish! List five things you can thank God for—and then thank Him!

1.

2.

3.

4.

5.

We're thankful that you're sticking with this news assignment—and we know God is pleased when you spend time with Him studying His Word. You can belong to God's club—the club of those who follow God by learning His Word and obeying it.

HELP! HELP!

We've seen that Jonah realizes that God listens and cares; that God provides and is powerful; and that God rules. God is ruler over everything and everyone. That means you can look to Him for help and strength as you work to meet another *Testimony Times* deadline and any other challenges you're facing. He'll take care of you just as He took care of Jonah.

And how is Jonah doing?

Look again at your Observation Worksheets and find words that suggest what Jonah was feeling during his...uh...fishing trip!

Jonah 2:2 WHAT was Jonah feeling when he called out for help to the Lord?

_____

Jonah 2:9 HOW was Jonah going to sacrifice to God?

_____

Somehow, as he sat in the fish's stomach, Jonah moved from crying for help to having a "voice of thanksgiving" (verse 9). Let's figure out why he was able to take that big step.

Jonah 1:2 WHAT had God told Jonah to do?

_____

Jonah 1:3 WHAT had Jonah done in response to God's command?

_____

Disobedience brings consequences, and Jonah seems to be very aware that God could have let him die. But Jonah is thankful that God is merciful. Mercy means not giving someone the punishment they deserve. That's why Jonah raised a voice of thanksgiving!

By the way, are you merciful to others? Do you try not to get somebody back even when they've hurt you? If you want to follow God, you need to learn to be merciful.

"LORD, TEACH ME TO PRAY"

Jonah's prayer is a very typical Hebrew prayer. It contains many of the elements common to Jewish prayer. Four of those elements are listed below:

(**A**)**doration** is praising God for who He is.

(**C**)**onfession** is admitting things you've done and said that you shouldn't have. It's also admitting things you should have done and said but didn't do.

(**T**)**hanksgiving** is telling God you're grateful for the things He's done for you and the blessings He's given.

(**S**)**upplication** means asking God to help you or someone else.

Adoration, confession, thanksgiving, and supplication—the first letters of these four words spell "ACTS." That simple word is a great way to remember one way to pray. Try praying through these four steps these next few weeks while you're on the Joppa-Nineveh news desk.

A PRAYER FROM THE HEART

It took a lot of courage for Jonah to pray from the belly of a fish. Practice your memory verse by filling in the blanks below.

I will _____ to You

With a voice of _____.

That which I have vowed I will _____.

_____ is from the Lord.

Jonah _____:_____

A MERCIFUL JUDGE

Can you think of a time in your life when you deserved to be punished, but you received mercy instead? That's what the Christian life is all about—and that could be an important point to raise in your *Testimony Times* story.

God is holy and must punish sin. We are all sinners (Romans 3:23). We sin when we break God's commandments. Sin is knowing what is right and good but not doing it! When we disobey Mom or Dad, that's a sin. When we aren't loving to our brothers and sisters or kind to our friends, that's a sin. When we don't tell the truth, that's a sin.

God punishes sin—but in His mercy He punished Jesus for your sin instead of punishing you. When you admit that you're a sinner and when you believe that Jesus is God's Son and that He died on the cross for your sin, you're ready to ask Him to be your Savior and Lord. And you won't be punished for your sin! Now that's a reason to be thankful!

Jonah knew he had done wrong—and knows only God can save him. That is why Jonah says, "Salvation is from the Lord" (Jonah 2:9). By the way, do you know that only Jesus can save us from our sins?

WISH YOU WERE HERE . . .

Today's the day we hope for a photo op (as in "OPportunity"), but it's going to be hard to get the right one.

> Jonah 2:1 WHERE is Jonah as he prays the prayer he's been sharing with you?

The WHERE question you just answered gives us a chance to talk about an important investigative tool called *context*. When you study the Bible, it's very important to understand the context of a passage. Context is the setting in which something is told or found. For instance, where would you find a bed in your house? What about a refrigerator? A bedroom is the context for a bed. And a kitchen is the context for a refrigerator. When you look at context in the Bible, you look at the verses surrounding the passage you're studying. You also think about where the passage fits in the big picture of the whole Bible. Context includes:

- The place where something happens
- The time an event occurs
- The customs of the group of people involved
- The time in history an event occurred

Sometimes you can discover all these things from just the verses you're studying. Sometimes you have to study other passages of

Scripture. It's always important to be on the lookout for context because it helps you discover what the Bible is saying.

Using the following questions as cues, describe what you think it might be like in the stomach of a fish.

What might Jonah be smelling?

_____

How much room does he have to stretch out?

_____

What might be available for Jonah to eat?

_____

How much light gets in?

_____

Is there a timer or a calendar to let Jonah know when he's going to get out?

_____

How would you feel in the situation you just described?

_____

_____

_____

The context (the stomach of a fish) of Jonah's song of praise and thanksgiving makes his words really something awesome!

Photo Shoot

Before writing your story tomorrow, do your best to get a photo to run with it. Be creative and, in the space provided, draw a picture from Jonah 2.

As you finish your study today, keep in mind Jonah's example and give thanks to God for whatever stinky circumstances you find yourself in right now!

Going to Press

Coming to you now from the belly of a fish, the next installment of the Jonah story! Let us know what you have to say!

First, the headline. What's a good head for Jonah 2? Write it on the line provided on the next page.

It's time to go to press, so either write your own story for the *Testament Times* or fill in the blanks and add your thoughts to the article that we've started for you.

TESTIMONY TIMES

ISSUE 3   VOL 3

BIG NEWS!

Put your headline here.

fter being tossed

_____
where (Jonah 1:15)

and swallowed by a

_____ ,
what (Jonah 1:17)

Jonah remained there for

_____ .
how long (Jonah 1:17)

Perhaps not surprisingly he spent much of that time

_____ .
doing what (Jonah 2:1)

Perhaps very surprisingly, though, Jonah's was a prayer of

_____ .
what (Jonah 2:9)

During his time in the great fish, this reporter suggests that Jonah realized his s ___ ___ of disobedience and God's m ___ ___ ___ ___ in not letting

him die in the storm at sea. In a miraculous demonstration of His power, God used a great fish to save His disobedient servant. But my report doesn't end here.

After Jonah, who was trying to run away from God, spent three days and nights in a fish's stomach, the fish

_____

_____ .
what (Jonah 2:10)

Credit is given to

_____
who (Jonah 2:10)

for prompting this act of mercy. What an awesome God!

What impact this amazing event will have on Wrong Way Jonah remains to be seen. Don't miss next week's edition of the *Testimony Times*!

Great work! And super cliffhanger! Readers can hardly wait to see what Jonah's life inside a fish will now mean for life on the outside!

"EXTRA! EXTRA!"

A Prayer Journal

You'll need:

> Two sheets of 8 1/2 x 11-inch cardboard
> Several pieces of 8 1/2 x 11-inch white paper
> Fabric, white glue, and scissors or paint and brushes
> A pencil
> Colored pencils or pens
> A hole punch
> Some ribbon, yarn, or shoe laces

1. Cover the cardboard with fabric or paint it.
2. After the covers are dry, you can draw or paint designs on them.
3. Punch three holes into the covers and the white paper.
4. Place the paper between your decorated cardboard covers.
5. Insert the ribbon, yarn, or shoe laces into the holes and tie securely in a bow or knot.

A prayer journal is a place to keep track of your prayers—and of God's answers. You can write entire prayers or just a phrase or two: Tell God what happened today and what you need help with. When God answers, make a note of it in your book. You might want to have dates beside both the requests and the answers.

It's great to look back through a prayer journal at the end of the year and praise God for all the times He so clearly answered your prayers.

Songs of Praise

Many songs you sing in church or Sunday school can be used as prayers. If you don't know the songs that follow, add some of your favorites to each category. Use these songs as you pray through ACTS.

Adoration: "Praise the Name of Jesus"
"Great Is the Lord"
"I Love You, Lord"

_____

_____

_____

Confession: "Create in Me a Clean Heart"

_____

_____

_____

Thanksgiving: "Lord, I Lift Your Name on High"

_____

_____

_____

Supplication: "In My Life, Lord, Be Glorified"
"Take My Life"

_____

_____

_____

Chimes from Under the Sea

You'll need a two-liter plastic bottle, scissors, a hole punch, an electric drill, small drill bits, 16-20 seashells, fishing line, twine—and an adult to help.

1. Cut a 3-inch wide ring from the plastic bottle.
2. Punch 4 holes, evenly spaced, around the top and bottom edge of the plastic ring.
3. Carefully drill small holes in the seashells. Drill slowly or the shells will break.
4. Cut 4 lengths of fishing line into varying lengths of between 10 and 18 inches.
5. Insert the fishing line into the holes along the bottom edge of the plastic ring. Tie a secure knot.
6. Then tie 4 or 5 shells on each fishing line.
7. Cut 4 lengths of twine into 18-inch pieces.
8. Tie the twine into the 4 holes on the top of the plastic ring.
10. Tie the ends of the twine together in a knot. Use the knot as a hanger.

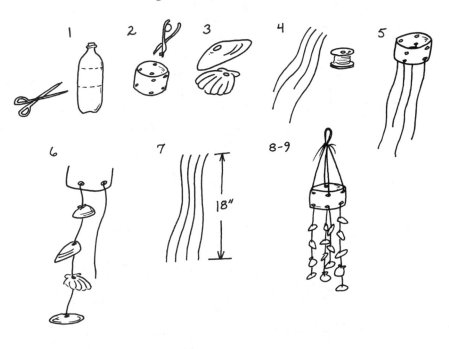

4

JONAH 3

Your Assignment

So did Jonah's time in the belly of a fish change his heart? The readers of the *Testimony Times* are eager to know what happens. It's not every day that God puts a man in the belly of a great fish that vomits him up on shore three days later.

▼

GETTING YOUR BEARINGS

As Jonah's adventures continue, you're going to follow him to the city of Nineveh. Going to that big city will give you lots of opportunities to ask your journalism questions: WHO, WHAT, WHERE, WHEN, WHY, and HOW. You'll want to get the facts straight for your readers!

Jonah 3:1-2 WHAT is happening?

_____

_____

Jonah 3:1 Has it happened before? _____ WHEN? (See
Jonah 1:1 if you need help.)

_____

Jonah 3:3 WHAT does Jonah do this time?

_____

Thinking back to what you've read in chapters 1-2,
WHY do you think Jonah does what he does this time?

_____

WHAT would you do if you were Jonah and WHY?

_____

WHY?

_____

Good job! You've got some good material for your newspaper article. We're heading to Nineveh to get the rest of the
story! We have to travel hundreds of miles to get there. That's
a long way for "Wrong Way Jonah"!

NEWS YOU CAN USE

God loves it when people turn from their wicked ways. In this week's memory verse, the king of Nineveh urges his people to change how they are treating others.

Let men call on God earnestly that each may turn from his wicked way and from the violence which is in his hands.

—Jonah 3:8

Write these words on an index card and read through them a few times before you're back to work tomorrow! (Are you praying using ACTS—Ⓐdoration, Ⓒonfession, Ⓣhanksgiving, Ⓢupplication?)

DAY 2

AN INTERVIEW WITH THE HEAD HONCHO

Have you ever found yourself saying, like grown-ups say, "I'm up against a wall"? To be up against a wall means you are in a hard situation. Things are tough—hard to get over or around.

Don't you think Jonah kind of felt his back was up against a wall? He didn't want to go to Nineveh, but he also didn't want to take another ride in the stomach of a great fish!

Your readers need to understand why Jonah didn't want to go to Nineveh.

Read Jonah 3:2-3. WHAT important fact about the city do you find in both verses? HOW many days would it take to walk through it? Write your answers on the notepad below.

FACTS ON NINEVEH

Do you remember what you learned about Nineveh when God first told Jonah to go there? Read Jonah 1:2 and add those facts to your notepad.

HOOFiNG iT

How far can you get in "three days"?

If you were traveling alone on fast horses, like the Pony Express, you'd get about 225 miles.

If you were with a big group, say on the Oregon Trail, you could probably cover 33 miles.

If you were in a car (and obeying the speed limit!), you'd put on 1,650 miles.

If you were traveling alone and on foot, you'd walk about 60 miles.

Now that Jonah's in Nineveh, the story really gets interesting! Read Jonah 3:3-9. WHO are the main people involved in this story? Unscramble their names below.

NOHAJ _____

ELPPOE FO VENNIHE _____

GKIN FO HINEVNE _____

As a reporter, you want to go straight to the top for an interview, and who could be higher than the king? Boy, that would be a scoop! From reading Jonah 3:3-9, how do you think the king would answer the following questions?

WHAT, O King, has Jonah told you is going to happen?

_____

Did he tell you WHEN?

_____

Do you know WHO is going to do this to Ninevah and WHY?

_____

_____

I noticed, O King, you're dressed differently today. WHAT did you do when you heard Jonah's message?

_____

WHAT four things did you tell the people to do? (Check out Jonah 3:7-8.)

1. _____

2. _____

3. _____

4. _____

HOW did you let the people know what to do?

_____

WHAT did you hope would happen because of your proclamation?

_____

Wow, King, what a day you had! Can I quote you?
(Write out verses 8 and 9—they'll really add punch to
your story!)

_____

_____

_____

_____

_____

What a scoop! *You* just got the facts from the *king*, of all
people! Great going!

Fashion Trends in Nineveh

Yesterday, you interviewed the king. You saw that he and
his people called for a fast and there was a run on sackcloth.
Sackcloth was definitely the thing to wear that day! On your
Observation Worksheet, mark every time "sackcloth" is used
in Jonah 3:1-9. You could just draw a black 👕 like this over
the word.

ITCHY DUDS

Sackcloth was a warm, dark material woven from goat or camel hair. Garments made of sackcloth felt rough and itchy against a person's skin. Sackcloth was worn to show sorrow for sins, its harsh texture reminding people of how uncomfortable sin should be to us. When people wore sackcloth and put ashes on their skin, they usually fasted as well. That means they chose not to eat food and/or drink liquids.

Sackcloth, ashes, and fasting were outward expressions of a heart full of sorrow for wrong choices and sin.

"Fast" is an important word like "sackcloth." Turn to your Observation Worksheet. See if you can find this key word in Jonah 3:1-9, once where the actual word "fast" is used and then again where it is described. Mark both places and record them below:

verse _____

verse _____

The head office of the *Testimony Times* is begging for a picture. They want to run it in full-color, so draw the best picture you can that shows what is happening in Nineveh according to Jonah 3:4-9.

That was the most amazing picture the *Testimony Times* ever received from a reporter! Excellent work! We're so proud of you!

OFF THE HOOK

Wow! The king and his people showed God they were really sorry for all the wrong things they had done. Do you remember what the king hoped God would do? Let's find out exactly what happened by reading the last verse of chapter 3. It's really great.

Read Jonah 3:10. Do you see a key word that you marked in Jonah 1:7? Mark it here too.

There's another tough word in this verse. Do you know what the word "relent" means? In this case, it means God didn't do what Jonah had told the people He would do.

According to Jonah 3:10, WHY didn't God do what He said He was going to do?

_____

How would you feel if you were one of the Ninevites?

_____

A PUZZLING ASSIGNMENT

The newspaper wants to run a crossword puzzle with your article, but the editor-in-chief needs you to do it first to make sure all the answers are right. See if you can answer the questions without looking at the verses. Of course, they're there if you need them!

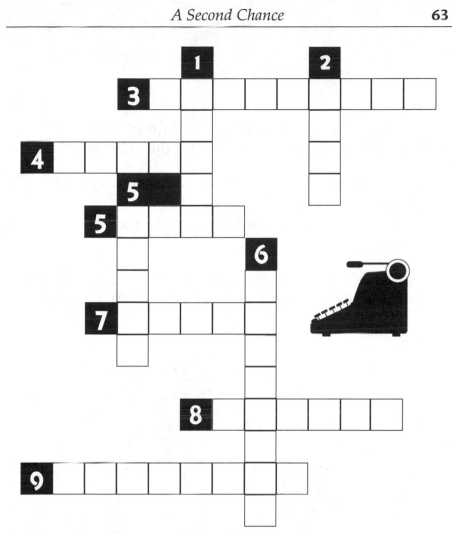

ACROSS

3. What did the Ninevites wear to show they had repented? (Jonah 3:5)
4. Who called the people of Nineveh back to God? (Jonah 3:4)
5. What did the Ninevites call to show they were sorry for their wickedness? (Jonah 3:5)
7. How many days did it take to walk through the city of Nineveh? (Jonah 3:3)
8. What did the Ninevites fear they would do if they didn't repent? (Jonah 3:9)

9. What did God do when He saw the Ninevites' acts of repentance? (Jonah 3:10)

DOWN
1. What did the repentant king sit on? (Jonah 3:6)
2. Who told Jonah what to tell the people of Nineveh? (Jonah 3:3)
5. In how many days would God overthrow Nineveh? (Jonah 3:4)
6. How did the people respond to Jonah's message? (Jonah 3:5)

Hey, what's the memory verse this week? Practice now— and tomorrow you can work on getting a photo for your story.

DAY 5

▼

GOING TO PRESS

Uh oh! The people who type in all the articles at the paper had their fingers on the wrong keys when they typed in your memory verse for the week. See if you can decode the message below. You can use the key on the next page.

O v g n v m x z o o l m T l w
___ ___ ____ __ ___

v z i m v h g o b g s z g v z x s
__ _____ ____ ____

n z b g f i m u i l n s r h d r x p v w
___ ____ ____ ___ _____

d z b z m w u i l n g s v e r l o v m x v
___ ___ ____ ___ _____

d s r x s r h r m s r h s z m w h.
_____ __ __ ___ _____.

—Q l m z s 3:8
_____

KEY

A = Z	G = T	M = N	S = H	Y = B
B = Y	H = S	N = M	T = G	Z = A
C = X	I = R	O = L	U = F	
D = W	J = Q	P = K	V = E	
E = V	K = P	Q = J	W = D	
F = U	L = O	R = I	X = C	

Why don't you see if you can say this verse out loud to your mom or dad? Don't forget to say where it's found in the Bible.

The editors at the *Testimony Times* are calling again. They need your story right away! They want to beat the other newspapers to the streets. Yours will be the lead article, the very first one in the paper. But first you need a headline for your story. What have we been talking about all week? That's your headline! Write it in the blank on the next page.

TESTIMONY TIMES

ISSUE 4   VOL 4

BIG NEWS!

_____

Put your headline here.

After a false start, the Hebrew   prophet

_____
who (Jonah 3:3)

went to

_____
where (Jonah 3:3)

to tell the people that in

_____
how many (Jonah 3:4)

days their city would be overthrown. The response was amazing. People throughout the large city of Nineveh called a

_____
what (Jonah 3:5)

and put on

_____.
what (Jonah 3:5)

Although not among the first to hear Jonah's message, the king acted quickly when he learned about the Jew's warning. Taking off his royal

_____ ,
what (Jonah 3:6)

he covered himself with sackcloth and sat on ashes. The king acted on the urgent situation by issuing a

_____
what (Jonah 3:7)

that stopped beasts, herds, and flocks as well as human beings from eating and drinking. Likewise, animals as well as humans were commanded to put on sackcloth, and the king called his people to

_____
what (Jonah 3:8)

The king had acted on the hope that the God Jonah spoke for would be kind to the people of Nineveh and withdraw His

_____
what (Jonah 3:9)

and let them live—and that's exactly what happened! God did not bring on the

_____
what (Jonah 3:10)

He had declared He would bring.

EXTRA! EXTRA!

Please Come!

Jonah was a missionary to people who did not know the one true God whom Jonah served. Like Jonah, you can be a missionary in your own neighborhood or school. Start by choosing an event at church that you could invite a friend to. Find out the details (what, where, when, and the other W's and an H) and then make an invitation. First, fold a piece of construction paper in half and write "You Are Invited!" on the front. Then decorate it with felt pens, crayons, stickers, or fabric scraps. On the inside, include all the information about the activity that your friend and his or her parents would need to know: the title of the event; the name, address, and phone number of your church; the date and time of the event; and your name, address, and phone number. You might want to ask your parents to drive you and your friend. If they agree, put in your invitation something like, "My parents will drive us!"

Playin' Around

This week's story would make a great play for you and your friends to put on for your families. Look at all the fun characters you could play. You could be Jonah, or the king, or people from Nineveh, or even the animals, who also had to wear sackcloth and ashes. Don't forget to make lots of animal noises when you perform your play. Have fun!

5

J O N A H   4

Your Assignment

This week you're going to interview Jonah. We're wondering how he feels about everything that happened in Nineveh.

A CHANGE OF HEART

It's time for your Observation Worksheets and a final search for key words. Read Jonah 4 and mark these key words. (If you marked these key words in other chapters, be sure to use the same colors or symbols you used earlier.)

Jonah   Lord *or* God   appointed

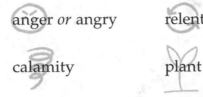

anger *or* angry   relent *or* relented

calamity   plant

Today you're going to look back at Jonah 3:10. WHAT didn't God do that He said He was going to do?

_____

If you were Jonah, how do you think you would feel about God's change of heart?

_____

STRAIGHT FROM THE PROPHET'S MOUTH

The editors of the *Testimony Times* think your readers will only believe what they're about to read if it comes straight from the prophet himself, so you're going to have to interview Jonah. He may be a little grumpy today, so watch out. If you read Jonah 3:10 and 4:1-3 very carefully, you'll be able to answer the interview questions.

"Jonah, how did you feel when God didn't do what He said He was going to do?"

4:1 _____ and_____

4:3 _____

"Why didn't you go to Nineveh the first time?"

_____

"Wow, that's an honest answer. What did you think you would forestall—that is, put off—if you went to Tarshish instead?" (Hint: What does "this" in verse 4:2 refer to? Check out verse 3:10 as well.)

_____

"In your prayer to the Lord, you say a lot about who God is. What are some of the ways you describe Him?"

_____

"Thank you, Mr. Jonah. You were a tough interview, but we've got some really good material for the readers of the *Testimony Times* now!"

Now let's contrast Jonah's reaction to the situation with God's response. A contrast shows how two things are different or opposite. The Bible uses many contrasts, such as "light" and "dark" or "truth" and "lie." List the words that describe the differences.

Jonah	**God**
Jonah 4:1	Jonah 4:2

_____   _____

_____

_____

_____

A BAD ATTITUDE DOES NO GOOD

You may have thought that Jonah got on the boat to Tarshish because he was afraid of the Ninevites, or because he didn't want to obey God for some other reason. But in verse 2, he tells us that he didn't want to go to the wicked Ninevites because he knew God would be compassionate and kind, and he wanted God to punish them!

In verse 4, God asks Jonah a very important question. What is it?

_____

Think about how Jonah might answer that question, and we'll talk more about it tomorrow. Good work today!

A PROPHET'S TESTIMONY

A good journalist needs statements from eyewitnesses, and that's what this week's memory verse is. The prophet Jonah declares something that he knows about God. There's no better choice for a memory verse than this powerful statement by Jonah himself!

You are a gracious and compassionate God,
slow to anger and abundant in lovingkindness,
and one who relents concerning calamity.
—Jonah 4:2

Write these lines on an index card and start memorizing. These are wonderful truths to have hidden away in your heart!

MADE IN THE SHADE

When we left God and Jonah, the Lord had just asked Jonah a question.

Jonah 4:4 WHAT did God ask Jonah?

_____

Jonah 4:5 WHAT did Jonah say in response? (Yes, this is a trick question!)

_____

Jonah 4:5 WHERE did Jonah go?

_____

Have you ever been so mad about something that you walked away, sat down, folded your arms, and just sat there? The next time you get angry you might want to stop and talk with God about it. Tell Him what you're angry about and then ask Him what He wants you do do.

Jonah built himself a shelter so he would have shade from the sun.

Jonah 4:5 WHAT was he waiting to see?

_____

A key word that is important to the story, although it doesn't appear as frequently as other key words we've seen, is the word "appointed." That means "sent to do a specific task." It also shows up in Jonah 1! List what God appointed in each verse below. (Did you get this key word marked in all these verses?)

Jonah 1:17 _____

Jonah 4:6 _____

Jonah 4:7 _____

Jonah 4:8 _____

GOD'S ANGER VS. OUR ANGER

Another contrast! We can learn a lot about ourselves and about God by contrasting what makes Him angry with what makes us angry. Take a look at where you marked the key word "anger" or "angry" in chapter 4.

WHAT makes Jonah angry?

Jonah 4:8-9_____

WHAT makes God angry?

Jonah 3:8-9 _____

Do you know what God means when He talks about the "violence which is in a person's hands"? It's when someone uses his hands to hurt another person. God created us, and He doesn't want us hurting what He created.

People who do evil things provoke God's anger. We make God angry when we turn our backs on Him, when we live as if *we* are in charge and ignore Him. But what good news about God's anger does your memory verse this week offer?

_____

_____

isn't it obvious?

Well, Jonah is angry. Is God, too? Learn what's going on so you can let the *Testimony Times* readers know!

The story of Jonah ends somewhat suddenly. God asks a question that has an obvious answer. Read Jonah 4:9-11.

Jonah 4:9 WHAT straightforward question does God ask Jonah?

_____

Jonah 4:9 WHAT answer does Jonah give to God's question?

_____

A good reporter always asks *why?* So let's see why Jonah is upset about a plant! You marked "plant" every time it was used in Jonah 4. List the facts about the plant.

Jonah 4:6

_____

Jonah 4:7

_____

Jonah 4:8 (WHAT happened when the plant died?)

_____

Jonah 4:10

_____

Now then, do you think Jonah has a good reason to be angry? WHY?

_____

Jonah 4:11 WHAT question does God ask Jonah?

_____

When God asks this question, what does He want Jonah to see?

_____

Contrasts help us get a point across and see what's important. We've got a clear contrast here in Jonah 4. Look at the word "compassion" in verse 10.

Jonah 4:10 WHAT did *Jonah* have compassion on?

_____

Now look at the word "compassion" in verse 11.

Jonah 4:11 WHAT did *God* have compassion on?

_____

Which is more important? Put a cross over the right answer.

Jesus died for people, not for plants! God doesn't want people to perish (to go to hell). That's why He sent Jesus to die for our sins—so we could be forgiven and go to heaven and live with God forever.

God didn't want the people of Nineveh to perish, so He sent Jonah to warn the people. And it worked! The people repented (had a change of mind) and turned from their wicked and violent ways.

Jonah didn't understand God's heart. He was more concerned about his feelings than God's. Jonah was thankful for God's compassion and lovingkindness when it applied to him (Jonah 2:9 and 4:2), but he was not so excited when God showed it to people Jonah considered his enemies (the Ninevites).

The wrong-way prophet reacted the wrong way to God's kindness toward Nineveh! When Jonah finally obeyed God and called the residents of the city to repentance, they listened and responded—and then as you saw, Jonah got angry when God didn't punish the folks who had looked to the Lord for forgiveness.

Why did God report this true story in the Bible? It's so we won't be like Jonah. In this week's assignment, Jonah cared more about his own comfort than he did about the people. But God cared more about the people. He wanted them to know what would happen if they didn't turn away from their wickedness and about His love and forgiveness if they did!

GETTING THE RIGHT SHOT

It's photo time! Draw a series of pictures that reflects the twist with which the book of Jonah ends. Jonah 4:5-8 suggests four photos!

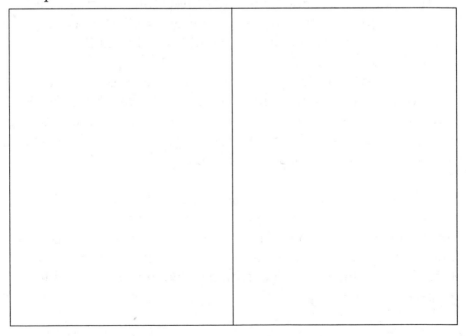

A WHALE OF A TALE

We're going to test your powers of memory as a reporter. How much do you remember of Jonah's exciting tale? Play this game with a friend or family member and find out!

WHAT YOU'LL NEED: The game board on the next page, a coin to flip, and a marker for each player. You can use Monopoly markers or Jelly Belly Beans or buttons.

HOW TO PLAY: Flip a coin. Heads, you move two spaces. Tails, you move one space. If you land on a memory-verse square, say the verse and get a free turn. First player to reach

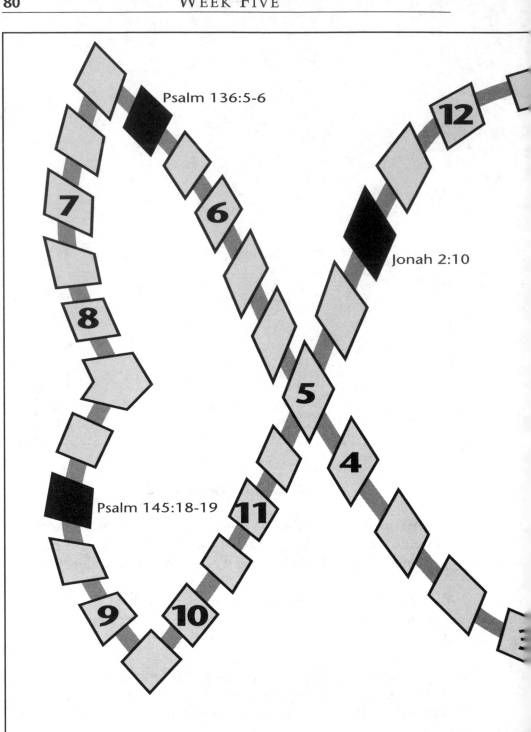

Psalm 136:5-6

12

Jonah 2:10

7

6

8

5

4

Psalm 145:18-19

11

9

10

13 **14** Jonah 3:8

15

Jonah 4:2

The word of the Lord came to Jonah—move ahead three spaces

Jonah went the wrong way to Tarshish—go back to the beginning

Captain tells Jonah to pray—move ahead one space

Sailors cast lots. Lots fall on Jonah—move back one space

Jonah tells the truth about his faith in God—move ahead two spaces

Jonah tells the sailors to throw him into the sea—move ahead three spaces

The sailors pray to Jonah's God—move ahead one space

The Lord appointed a great fish to swallow Jonah—move ahead four spaces

The fish vomits Jonah onto the dry land—move ahead one space!

Jonah obeys God and goes to Nineveh—move ahead three spaces

Nineveh repents—move ahead three spaces

Jonah becomes angry—move back five spaces

The plant grows and Jonah's happy—move ahead three spaces

The plant dies and Jonah's mad—move back three spaces

God asks Jonah a question and learns a good lesson—go to the finish: You win!

You Win!

2 **1** ◄ **Start Here**

Nineveh with a good attitude wins!

You're on the final deadline with this writing assignment. Our readers will be sad to see it come to an end. You've worked hard, and we've all learned so much!

DAY
5

▼

GOING TO PRESS

The readers of the *Testimony Times* have been waiting to see how the story ends. Who would have predicted Jonah's attitude after the Ninevites repented and God relented? We know you'll come up with a great headline for this install-ment of the Jonah story. Write it in the line on the next page.

TESTIMONY TIMES

ISSUE 5   VOL 5

BIG NEWS!

Put your headline here.

As reported earlier, God saw evidence of the Ninevites' repentance. He relented and did not bring on the

_____
what (Jonah 3:10)

He had declared He would inflict. In response, Jonah went

_____
where (Jonah 4:5)

and built a shade cover for himself as he waited to see

_____.
what (Jonah 4:5)

Acting in mercy, God increased Jonah's shade by providing a

_____.
what (Jonah 4:6)

Jonah's pleasure at the gift immediately disappeared the next morning when God appointed a

_____.
what (Jonah 4:7)

It_____ the plant,
what (Jonah 4:7)

and the plant

_____.
what (Jonah 4:7)

Jonah, who wanted to live when the fish swallowed him, was now so miserable he wanted to die. Jonah then heard God ask him

_____.
what (Jonah 4:9)

Not at all humbled by his underwater adventure in the belly of a fish, Jonah declared that his anger was justified.

It is reported that God used the vine, its withering, and Jonah's angry reaction to try to remind Jonah that people's lives—even sinful people like the Ninevites—are more valuable than the plant. "Should I not have

_____
what (Jonah 4:11)

on Nineveh, the great city in which there are more than 120,000 persons?" asked God.

Best efforts to research what happened next in Jonah's life have been fruitless. Perhaps the fruit will come in the lives of those who read about Jonah and learn not to go the wrong way.

A Big Finish

Sometimes reporters learn a lot about themselves when they work on a big story. They often jot down their thoughts in their personal notebooks. Jonah is such a great true story that we wanted you to have that chance too. Write down some of the things *you* learned on this assignment. There's so much more to it than just a man being swallowed by a big fish!

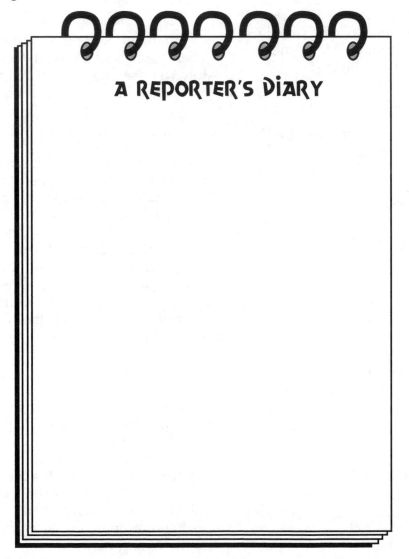

A REPORTER'S DIARY

EXTRA! EXTRA!

Flicker Animation Book

What one scene from your assignment is still sharp in your mind? You can make a Flicker Animation Book to make that scene come to life. You'll need cardboard, 30 pieces of paper, scissors, a hole punch, a pencil, felt pens or colored pencils, ribbon, gumstrip or rubber cement, and a brush.

Cut the paper into 3x2½-inch strips. You'll need one piece of cardboard that size. Punch two holes into the left-hand side of the paper strips and the cardboard back. On the paper between the two holes, write the page numbers 1 to 30.

On the right-hand side of each piece of paper, lightly draw with pencil a guideline or box. Be sure that the guidelines or boxes are on the same place on each piece of paper.

Draw a simple cartoon character on page one. Then, on each following page, draw a slight variation of that character or scene to show movement. Put the pages of your Flicker Animation Book in order from 1 to 30. Put the cardboard back under your booklet.

Insert the ribbon into the holes and tie it securely. Brush gumstrip on the left-hand side of the pages to hold them securely in place. Now flick your Flicker Animation Book to watch a scene from the Jonah story unfold.

You can use this to tell people about Jonah—and about God who loves them and doesn't want them to perish. As you tell others about how they can repent and believe in Jesus Christ, you'll be God's right-way messenger!

A FINAL WORD FROM THE *TESTIMONY TIMES* EDITORS

You've done a terrific job! You've worked hard each step of the way.

You've learned some great things about God. You've seen His power and His love. You've seen His faithfulness even when we, like Jonah, aren't faithful or obedient. You've learned how to study and discover God's Word for yourself by asking questions using the 5 Ws and an H.

Most of all, we hope your study has encouraged you to go the right way in obedience to God. A God who is strong, kind, and in charge. A God who hears prayers and answers them. A God who is pleased when you trust and obey Him.

We're so proud of you. If you'll fill out the card in the back of this book and mail it to us, we'll send you something special. And we look forward to doing another study with you soon!

PUZZLE ANSWERS

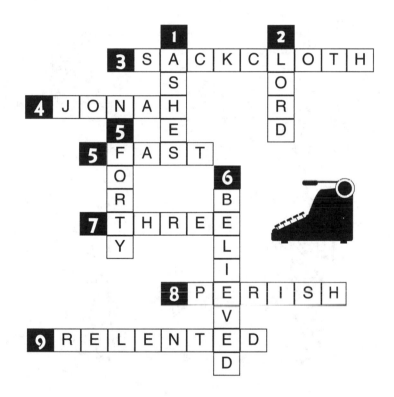

3 SACKCLOTH

4 JONAH

5 FAST

7 THREE

8 PERISH

9 RELENTED

1. ASHESEL
2. LORD
5. FORTY
6. BELIEVED

OBSERVATION WORKSHEETS
JONAH

Chapter 1

1 The word of the LORD came to Jonah the son of Amittai saying,

2 "Arise, go to Nineveh the great city and cry against it, for their wickedness has come up before Me."

3 But Jonah rose up to flee to Tarshish from the presence of the LORD. So he went down to Joppa, found a ship which was going to Tarshish, paid the fare and went down into it to go with them to Tarshish from the presence of the LORD.

4 The LORD hurled a great wind on the sea and there was a great storm on the sea so that the ship was about to break up.

5 Then the sailors became afraid and every man cried to his god, and they threw the cargo which was in the ship into the sea to lighten it for them. But Jonah had gone below into the hold of the ship, lain down and fallen sound asleep.

6 So the captain approached him and said, "How is it that you are sleeping? Get up, call on your god. Perhaps your god will be concerned about us so that we will not perish."

7 Each man said to his mate, "Come, let us cast lots so we may learn on whose account this calamity has struck us." So they cast lots and the lot fell on Jonah.

8 Then they said to him, "Tell us, now! On whose account has this calamity struck us? What is your occupation? And where do you come from? What is your country? From what people are you?"

9 He said to them, "I am a Hebrew, and I fear the LORD God of heaven who made the sea and the dry land."

10 Then the men became extremely frightened and they said to him, "How could you do this?" For the men knew that he was fleeing from the presence of the LORD, because he had told them.

11 So they said to him, "What should we do to you that the sea may become calm for us?"—for the sea was becoming increasingly stormy.

12 He said to them, "Pick me up and throw me into the sea. Then the sea will become calm for you, for I know that on account of me this great storm has come upon you."

13 However, the men rowed desperately to return to land but they could not, for the sea was becoming even stormier against them.

14 Then they called on the LORD and said, "We earnestly pray, O LORD, do not let us perish on account of this man's life and do not put innocent blood on us; for You, O LORD, have done as You have pleased."

15 So they picked up Jonah, threw him into the sea, and the sea stopped its raging.

16 Then the men feared the LORD greatly, and they offered a sacrifice to the LORD and made vows.

17 And the LORD appointed a great fish to swallow Jonah, and Jonah was in the stomach of the fish three days and three nights.

Chapter 2

1 Then Jonah prayed to the LORD his God from the stomach of the fish,

2 And he said,

  "I called out of my distress to the LORD,

  And He answered me.

  I cried for help from the depth of Sheol;

  You heard my voice.

3 "For You had cast me into the deep,

  Into the heart of the seas,

  And the current engulfed me.

  All Your breakers and billows passed over me.

4 "So I said, 'I have been expelled from Your sight.

  Nevertheless I will look again toward Your holy temple.'

5 "Water encompassed me to the point of death.

  The great deep engulfed me,

  Weeds were wrapped around my head.

6 "I descended to the roots of the mountains.

  The earth with its bars was around me forever,

  But You have brought up my life from the pit, O LORD my God.

7 "While I was fainting away,

  I remembered the LORD,

  And my prayer came to You,

  Into Your holy temple.

8 "Those who regard vain idols

  Forsake their faithfulness,

9 But I will sacrifice to You,

  With the voice of thanksgiving.

  That which I have vowed I will pay.

  Salvation is from the LORD."

10 Then the LORD commanded the fish, and it vomited Jonah up onto the dry land.

Chapter 3

1 Now the word of the LORD came to Jonah the second time, saying,

2 "Arise, go to Nineveh the great city and proclaim to it the proclamation which I am going to tell you."

3 So Jonah arose and went to Nineveh according to the word of the LORD. Now Nineveh was an exceedingly great city, a three days' walk.

4 Then Jonah began to go through the city one day's walk; and he cried out and said, "Yet forty days and Nineveh will be overthrown."

5 Then the people of Nineveh believed in God; and they called a fast and put on sackcloth from the greatest to the least of them.

6 When the word reached the king of Nineveh, he arose from his throne, laid aside his robe from him, covered himself with sackcloth and sat on the ashes.

7 He issued a proclamation and it said, "In Nineveh by the decree of the king and his nobles: Do not let man, beast, herd, or flock taste a thing. Do not let them eat or drink water.

8 "But both man and beast must be covered with sackcloth; and let men call on God earnestly that each may turn from his wicked way and from the violence which is in his hands.

9 "Who knows, God may turn and relent and withdraw His burning anger so that we will not perish."

10 When God saw their deeds, that they turned from their wicked way, then God relented concerning the calamity which He had declared He would bring upon them. And He did not do it.

Chapter 4

1 But it greatly displeased Jonah and he became angry.

2 He prayed to the LORD and said, "Please LORD, was not this what I said while I was still in my own country? Therefore in order to forestall this I fled to Tarshish, for I knew that You are a gracious and compassionate God, slow to anger and abundant in lovingkindness, and one who relents concerning calamity.

3 "Therefore now, O LORD, please take my life from me, for death is better to me than life."

4 The LORD said, "Do you have good reason to be angry?"

5 Then Jonah went out from the city and sat east of it. There he made a shelter for himself and sat under it in the shade until he could see what would happen in the city.

6 So the LORD God appointed a plant and it grew up over Jonah to be a shade over his head to deliver him from his discomfort. And Jonah was extremely happy about the plant.

7 But God appointed a worm when dawn came the next day and it attacked the plant and it withered.

8 When the sun came up God appointed a scorching east wind, and the sun beat down on Jonah's head so that he became faint and begged with all his soul to die, saying, "Death is better to me than life."

9 Then God said to Jonah, "Do you have good reason to be angry about the plant?" And he said, "I have good reason to be angry, even to death." 10 Then the LORD said, "You had compassion on the plant for which you did not work and which you did not cause to grow, which came up overnight and perished overnight.

11 "Should I not have compassion on Nineveh, the great city in which there are more than 120,000 persons who do not know the difference between their right and left hand, as well as many animals?"

DISCOVER 4 YOURSELF!®

Kay Arthur and Cyndy Shearer
Kids "make" a movie to discover who Jesus is and His impact on their lives. Activities and 15-minute lessons make this study of John 1–10 great for all ages!

ISBN 978-0-7369-0119-2

Kay Arthur, Janna Arndt, Lisa Guest, and Cyndy Shearer
This book picks up where *Jesus in the Spotlight* leaves off: John 11–16. Kids join a movie team to bring the life of Jesus to the big screen in order to learn key truths about prayer, heaven, and Jesus.

ISBN 978-0-7369-0144-4

Kay Arthur and Janna Arndt
As "advice columnists," kids delve into the book of James to discover—and learn how to apply—the best answers for a variety of problems.

ISBN 978-0-7369-0148-2

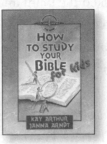

Kay Arthur and Janna Arndt
This easy-to-use Bible study combines serious commitment to God's Word with illustrations and activities that reinforce biblical truth.

ISBN 978-0-7369-0362-2

Kay Arthur and Janna Arndt
Focusing on John 17–21, children become "directors" who must discover the details of Jesus' life to make a great movie. They also learn how to get the most out of reading their Bibles.

ISBN 978-0-7369-0546-6

Kay Arthur and Scoti Domeij
As "reporters," kids investigate Jonah's story and conduct interviews. Using puzzles and activities, these lessons highlight God's loving care and the importance of obedience.

ISBN 978-0-7369-0203-8

Kay Arthur and Janna Arndt
Kids become archaeologists to uncover how God deals with sin, where different languages and nations came from, and what God's plan is for saving people (Genesis 3–11).

ISBN 978-0-7369-0374-5

Kay Arthur and Janna Arndt
God's Amazing Creation covers Genesis 1–2—those awesome days when God created the stars, the world, the sea, the animals, and the very first people. Young explorers will go on an archaeological dig to discover truths for themselves!

ISBN 978-0-7369-0143-7

Kay Arthur and Janna Arndt
The Lord's Prayer is the foundation of this special basic training, and it's not long before the trainees discover the awesome truth that God wants to talk to them as much as they want to talk to Him!

ISBN 978-0-7369-0666-1

Kay Arthur and Janna Arndt
Readers head out on the rugged Oregon Trail to discover the lessons Abraham learned when he left his home and moved to an unknown land. Kids will face the excitement, fears, and blessings of faith.

ISBN 978-0-7369-0936-5

Kay Arthur and Janna Arndt
Kids journey to God's heart using the inductive study method and the wonder of an adventurous spy tale.

ISBN 978-0-7369-1161-0

Kay Arthur and Janna Arndt
This engaging, high-energy study examines the journeys of Isaac, Jacob, and Esau and reveals how God outfits His children with everything they need for life's difficulties, victories, and extreme adventures.

ISBN 978-0-7369-0937-2

Kay Arthur and Janna Arndt
Kids explore the Bible Discovery Museum and solve the great mysteries about the future using the inductive study method and Revelation 1–7.

ISBN 978-0-7369-1527-4

Kay Arthur and Janna Arndt
Kids tackle Revelation 8–22 in this active and fun Bible study that explores what's to come and the importance of knowing Jesus.

ISBN 978-0-7369-2036-0

Books in the
New Inductive Study Series

〜〜〜〜

<table>
<tr><td>

Teach Me Your Ways
Genesis, Exodus,
Leviticus, Numbers, Deuteronomy

*Choosing Victory,
Overcoming Defeat*
Joshua, Judges, Ruth

Desiring God's Own Heart
1 & 2 Samuel,
1 Chronicles

Walking Faithfully with God
1 & 2 Kings, 2 Chronicles

*Overcoming Fear
and Discouragement*
Ezra, Nehemiah, Esther

*Trusting God
in Times of Adversity*
Job

*God's Answers for
Today's Problems*
Proverbs

*God's Blueprint
for Bible Prophecy*
Daniel

*Discovering the God
of Second Chances*
Jonah, Joel, Amos, Obadiah

*Finding Hope
When Life Seems Dark*
Hosea, Micah, Nahum,
Habakkuk, Zephaniah

</td><td>

*Opening the Windows
of Blessings*
Haggai, Zechariah, Malachi

The Call to Follow Jesus
Luke

*The Holy Spirit
Unleashed in You*
Acts

*God's Answers for
Relationships and Passions*
1 & 2 Corinthians

*Free from Bondage
God's Way*
Galatians, Ephesians

That I May Know Him
Philippians, Colossians

*Standing Firm in
These Last Days*
1 & 2 Thessalonians

*Walking in Power,
Love, and Discipline*
1 & 2 Timothy, Titus

*Living with Discernment
in the End Times*
1 & 2 Peter, Jude

God's Love Alive in You
1, 2, & 3 John,
Philemon, James

Behold, Jesus Is Coming!
Revelation

</td></tr>
</table>